ONE NATION, TWO WORLDS

Is America on the Brink of Civil War 2.0?

CONTENTS

INTRODUCTION

"The past explains how I got here, but the future is up to me – and I love to live life at full throttle."
--Janice Dickinson

Over the course of her tumultuous history, extending as far back to the signing of the Declaration of Independence to the current day, America has weathered the massive storms for which have shaken the core of her foundation. Since 1776, each generation of Americans has summoned both the strength and courage to master the obstacles that stand to lead us to our destiny. This summoning of relentless, unabashed American greatness has led us through the most unprecedented uncertainties imaginable: the first war to establish our independence as a sovereign people, the second war that would only begin to affirm a new reality of liberty and freedom for all citizens regardless of their skin color, both a world war and a cold war against totalitarian regimes that sent an entire globe to the brink of mass captivity, and the enduring battle within our own shores to establish greater justice, democratic representation across-the-board, and equal treatment under the law for every American citizen, all of which can be accounted for concerning the loss and physical destruction of countless lives here and abroad.

The summoning of America's greatness has led her through the darkest of economic despair on so many occasions, whether it would consist of the typical recession or widespread depression. The tenacity of our greatness continues to confront a deadly pandemic that shut down the world briefly and ended over one million American lives. Each time our greatness has been summoned upon, it has proven itself superior to all the trials and tribulations that stood to dismantle it. While there remains a great deal of work to be done in making our nation a more perfect union, there should be no doubt that no other society on Earth or throughout the entire history of mankind is a match for the formidable, unspeakable collective spirit of the American people. This unyielding collective American spirit, enriched by faith, guarded by conscience, tested by trials, and glorified in triumph, remains the greatest beacon of inspiration and promise for billions across the globe.

The reality of the challenges that so many previous generations endured will forever remain a secondhand reality in the minds of their posterity, but the legacies of their profound sacrifices remain as clear as day. The strength and courage upon which they summoned to reach for greater heights are deeply embedded in our spirit as a people. Our spirit encompasses, at its core, the once radical but longstanding, powerful conviction that each citizen should dictate the course of their own life and their own destiny as long as they do not infringe upon the human rights of others. Our spirit encompasses both a legal right and a moral authority to put forth a say in democracy; this is what extends the resources and tools to every American to redeem both the natural and unnatural imperfections of this nation, bringing us closer to that more perfect union in which aspire to be. Democracy extends ears to the many forgotten voices of the world, allowing them to be heard loud and clear through waves that echo from channel to channel until a new array of sunlight is their witness. Our republic stands to be forever destitute and meaningless if American democracy was to ever cease to endure.

Examining all the fundamental eras of darkness and despair that once ravaged across our land since the birth of our independence, none of them matches the growing national threat that presides before us. Our nation today is being tested by the wheels of fate like never before, and the course of action we assume on this day stands to have a lasting impact that could endure for generations to come. The threat for which lingers before us all is an alarmingly growing quest on the part of some in this country to seize political power at the vast expense of not only our collective spirit, but our collective will and moral conscience.

This threat to our nation transcends both ideological perspective and political party. The threat before us stands to overthrow representative American government as history knows it and replace it with one that resembles an authoritarian-style regime similar to former Nazi-fascism in Germany under Hitler and communist-totalitarianism in the former Soviet Union under Joseph Stalin. Most of us in this generation have never experienced political toxicity of this magnitude and have never imagined that such a threat could be even remotely possible in today's America.

What makes this threat so imminent and deadly is that its perpetrators and masterminds have incited violence and havoc consistently on their own fellow Americans in their quest to seize power, from Charlottesville to January 6th. Former president Donald Trump and his radical far right allies have proven countless times that they will stop at absolutely nothing to achieve their goal; they will declare enemies out of all those who refuse to pledge allegiance to their dangerous quest, issuing continued threats of violence as well as insurrectionist riots, seeking to overturn the results of democratically-won elections in the event of political shortcomings, and refusing to present evidence beyond a reasonable doubt to fully validate accusations of widespread fraud. The Trump-MAGA quest to overthrow American democracy is only part of the looming threat to our future.

An additional aspect of the Trump-MAGA threat consists of the blatant attempts in various states across the country to enact countless discriminatory laws attacking the right to vote, restricting a woman's autonomy over her own body and healthcare, and curtailing the constitutional and human rights of those in the LGBTQIAP community. These unfortunate courses of action are being followed by recently rising trends of homegrown acts of domestic terrorism and hate crimes against people of color, Jews, gays, lesbians, trans-men, and trans-women. All of this is the result of the increasing re-conformity among extremists in this country to racist, anti-Semitic, xenophobic, misogynistic, homophobic, and transphobic convictions, all which stem from the completely same foundation of bigotry, willful ignorance, injustice, and profound hate.

This is the same foundation that has destroyed and continues to destroy the gift of human life, resulting in death, violence, physical injury, a decline in mental health, the separation of loved ones, and disproportionate socio-economic and cultural oppression. If too many of us take this lightly and stand idly by as the radical far right Trump-MAGA cult continues its attempts to hijack our nation's greatness, replace it with an authoritarian form of government at both the federal and state levels, and reaffirm the white straight cisgender male paradigm of the past as the fundamental proprietor of political power, cultural dominance, and moral superiority, the prospects for a second civil war in the recognizable future will remain dangerously high and become only much worse.

It is critical for us all to confront the reality of division in this country and together reclaim the greatness of America's collective spirit. We must work together to discover the underlying roots of our differences on the surface and how most of us are truly not so different at the core. However, those who continue to denounce moral character as well as conscience, pledge allegiance to the destruction of our nation's identity, promote violence and division in the names of greed and political power, and advocate for the marginalization and destruction of Americans based on skin color, gender, culture, sexual orientation, and gender identity have proven themselves to not believe in unity nor honor our shared purpose and seem unbothered by the unraveling consequences of such actions.

The questions going forward are very simple: how can our generation work to overcome the Trump-MAGA cult in a lawfully, purely democratic fashion while averting the growing prospects for a nationally life-alerting second civil war? What must be done specifically to forever safeguard subsequent generations against such imminent threats so that they are prevented in their entirety, thus preserving the profound greatness of our collective American spirit?

1

Politics Is My Thing

"A noble leader answers not to the trumpet calls of self-promotion, but to the hushed whispers of necessity."

--Mollie Marti

During my former high school years, I earned a very strong and positive reputation among many.

While I was known very well for treating others with kindness and respect, exploring great lengths to maintain academic excellence, and remaining involved heavily in extra-curricular activities as well as community service initiatives, what I was known for greater than anything else was having a deep, abiding passion for political activism. It was during my high school journey when I began to achieve a great, in depth understanding of the various issues affecting the lives of Americans, particularly those of young people who remain often at the mercy of bullying, peer pressure, drug use, mental illness, and suicide. Countless young people across America today are also at the mercy of poverty and the lack of sound educational and economic opportunities, which are linked inextricably to the four issues mentioned previously. I sought to shine beacons of light and hope into the lives of many adolescents by emphasizing the importance of faith, education, hard work, self-assurance, and perseverance.

While seeking to make a difference in the lives of others through motivational speaking and anti-bullying advocacy brought sources of great pride and joy, I knew deep down inside that bestowing a meaningful and lasting impact on others' lives would involve a long-term re-assessment of public policy at every level. Making a positive difference on behalf of humanity, particularly children and adolescents, will involve honesty and humility followed by a non-partisan analysis concerning how policy shapes millions of lives from all backgrounds. This is what inspired my first run for public office. Never did I imagine, however, that it would take place only a few years after high school and less than one year after college.

A Political Journey in District 28

One of the questions I was asked by so many consisted of the following: "have you ever thought about running for office?" Some individuals would even ask me straightforwardly, "are you going to run for president some day?" To be asked these questions by so many in the first place was very inspiring but humbling at the same time. To be trusted with the task of leadership is to be trusted by the people with a boundless faith to maintain the utmost degree of character, integrity, decency, and morality, remembering that people and the betterment of their lives forever precedes self-interests. I would answer questions concerning a run for public office with a strong commitment to those I had served for years. It was during the end of 2014 when I had begun inquiring about the office of state representative in the 28th District back in Louisiana.

I was considering briefly to run in the 2015 election cycle; however, I had learned that the incumbent representative was eligible to run for a third and final term. I did not desire to run against the incumbent at that time, former Representative Robert Johnson, because I felt that he was an adequate leader for our district and had done well fighting for education, working families, and greater opportunities for all. Furthermore, it was not the most appropriate time to enter such a major political endeavor while still freshly into college and lacking the resources to finance the campaign. Instead, I decided to support incumbent Representative Johnson fully and volunteer for incumbent Mayor Kenneth Pickett, Sr. in my former hometown of Mansura, while focusing on my duties and responsibilities as a motivational speaker, author, an undergrad student at Louisiana State University at Alexandria, and an educator.

A year and a half later, during the spring of 2016, I was considering once again a run for the 28th District Louisiana legislature seat. This time incumbent Representative Johnson was not eligible for re-election in 2019, declaring the upcoming election cycle to be a wide-open field. The election would be nearly four years away, but it did not prevent me from testing the waters and inquiring into additional prospective candidates. A particular name that was being tossed in the atmosphere was Police Juror Kirby Roy, who was a former two-time candidate for the same legislature seat who ran against the incumbent in both 2007 and 2011 unsuccessfully. Another name that was being floated was local ranch owner Brian

Bordelon, who was the unsuccessful candidate against the incumbent in 2015.

Mr. Roy and I had known each other and maintained a positive relationship for years; I called him by phone to ask if he was considering a run for the seat, but he was not sure at the time. Mr. Bordelon and I had never met personally or had any contact by phone or on social media. Because there was still quite some time remaining before the election cycle in 2019, there had been no confirmed candidates for the upcoming season. Even I had remained discreet about my prospective run and only shared my plans and sought advice or information among very close confidants.

Over the next couple of years, I began considering prospective campaign managers and attempting to garner the early support of key influential individuals in the district. I also began to arouse the playing field on social media. Among the few close confidants whom I had consulted initially, I had their full support. In the summer of 2018, I had begun minimal rounds of neighborhood canvassing as well as meeting with local political, religious, and business leaders. As September approached, I purchased a twenty-minute segment on a local radio station, announcing my intention to run for the district's legislature seat.

I received enormous praise by many afterwards; radio consists of a fundamental media source in rural areas throughout the country. Just minutes prior to my radio announcement, I learned of two additional individuals who were considering a run for the seat. The individuals consisted of Donald Milligan and Daryl Deshotel. Milligan was a former educator, police juror, firefighter, and director of the local 911 center; Deshotel was a wealthy, local business owner. Both prospective candidates were white and much older than I was.

As the only person of color in the running for state representative in the 28th District, which is a rural area that is predominantly white and conservative, I could not help but wonder how greatly of a role in which race would play. The fact that I was well-known and admired highly by individuals of all races in the district brought minimal relief; this did not blind me, however, to the historically complicated reality of race relations that remains highly typical in many predominantly rural areas. I was also not blinded to the new reality of racism in many places; instead of the traditionally overt forms of racism that former generations endured, my generation is combatting discreetly closeted forms of bigotry and injustice that are often excused and misconstrued and continue without consequence. This issue will be assessed more in depth in a future chapter.

As I prepared to launch my campaign, I would ask many of my closest friends who happened to be white if most of the other whites they knew were racist, and all of them would tell me yes. Much to my dismay, they were brutally honest to me concerning my question. However, I did not allow this unfortunate news to bestow discouragement and instill layers of bitterness in my own aspirations. This also did not negatively impact my commitment to and love for all of God's children regardless of who they are and how they look. My specific concerns regarding the impact of skin color in the race only inspired me much more deeply to forward a political vision bounded in the causes of unity, shared purpose, content of character, and limitless opportunities for all the people who define the 28th District.

As the first few months of 2019 progressed, the race for state representative would reach full swing. During early spring, I encountered several obstacles that immediately ignited a burning fire beneath me to tackle like never before. One of the major obstacles before me consisted of name-recognition as a candidate. While I was well-known among a great deal of people throughout the district, I discovered that lots of more individuals had never heard of me. Milligan had district-wide recognition for decades of work throughout the community. Deshotel, who was initially unknown in the very beginning, skyrocketed his way to mainstream name-recognition due to his personal wealth. I, on the other hand, had much work to do.

Another obstacle standing before my candidacy consisted of my age. Milligan was approaching the age of seventy, while Deshotel enjoyed a youthful image in his mid-forties. Upon throwing my name in the hat, I was only twenty-five years of age. My former speech/drama teacher during high school as well as very close friend and mentor, KK Lemoine, informed me that my very young age would be a greater obstacle to victory than my skin color, and I was quite sure that many others would have agreed. As for the age versus race factor, my perspective was very simple: only time would tell.

An additional obstacle to the campaign consisted of the one thing that talks louder than humans ever could, which was money. As a Democrat, I expected the state and local party chapters to donate substantially to my campaign. Because Milligan was also running as a Democrat, however, the party chapters did not endorse nor offer financial assistance to any candidates in our race. I can still recall the day I learned of this as I leaned backwards against the wall in strong disarray. I wondered briefly if I should remain in the race even.

So, there I was. I was a twenty-five-year-old college grad and substitute teacher, running a campaign for state office that was widely unknown with little to no money to go forward. I also had no campaign manager, no staff, and no volunteers. As

I was leaning on the wall, staring forwardly across the room, I vowed to not quit, no matter how difficult the circumstances had become. I decided to keep moving forward because I realized that I was fighting on behalf of a cause much greater than myself. I also knew very strongly that I would never forgive myself later if I had given up. The only way forward was mapping out the greatest, most clear, and most realistic path to victory amid massive obstacles. My plan going forward was to install a strict grassroots campaign strategy that would defy the typical election-winning techniques hatched in the walls of wealth and special interests.

My new strategy consisted of three fundamental tenets: door-to-door canvassing, social media outreach, and face-to-face contact with voters. Because I had no flow of campaign contributions, I decided to exhaust an overwhelming majority of my substitute teaching paychecks on campaign literature and yard signs. Because I had no money to spare to boost social media expansion, I relied on friends for the sharing of content. I filmed multiple campaign commercial ads with the help of my brother, who is a professional photographer.

My first campaign ad garnered thousands of views over the course of just a few days. Many individuals in the district were very astonished and impressed; so many voters began to throw their support to my candidacy. This ad, alone, had given new life and purpose to a once dry, stagnant campaign. It would eventually shoot its way to television. After many months, the total number of views would reach beyond ten thousand views. While the additional commercials were not as prevalent as the first, they continued to pave the way for greater name recognition on my behalf. I also found myself being introduced into multiple district-wide community groups on social media, which also helped garner much support. Many of these individuals invited me into their homes for personal face-to-face conversations concerning my plans for office upon a prospective win on Election Day. I would also be invited to speak to certain venues about my candidacy. At many public events throughout the district, I would run into the other candidates in the race as well. The encounters were always friendly and cordial, as there was no ill feelings or animosity among us.

The greater social media presence carried the campaign a long way as I had begun door-to-door canvassing across the district. This was a day-to-day function of the campaign strategy. Every afternoon following a day of teaching, I began knocking on doors in a particular town chosen at random. As the summer season would approach, I had more time during the day in which to dedicate to knocking on voters' doors. I would spend anywhere between six to seven hours each day completing door-to-door canvassing. During some days in towns where there were greater acres of land in between homes, I would drive my car to the different homes. In towns where homes were more closely connected, I would park my car at a nearby gas station or grocery store and began canvassing the neighborhood by feet.

Many of these days were carried out during extreme temperatures in the upper 90s to lower 100s. I would be flowing with so much sweat that some voters would welcome me into their homes for a bit of time and offer bottles of water and cups of ice, which was deeply appreciated. Many voters were very glad to receive a home visit from political candidates, which had become a rare act of behavior in the district. I had received a great deal of support just from visiting voters' homes, giving them campaign literature, and talking to them concerning the issues affecting them daily. Most conversations would last anywhere between five to thirty minutes or possibly more. There was one voter whom I enjoyed a conversation with that lasted for a few hours. Many voters also recognized me from various signs stationed throughout the district.

During the final couple of months of campaigning, I began to receive a few campaign contributions from others. I received a contribution from a Louisiana Democratic organization dedicated to the issue of education. I also received door-to-door canvassing assistance from specific individuals in different towns, which garnered additional support simply on the strength of support from well-known figures who had the trust of those in their communities. I found myself stepping into a bit of controversy as I had begun calling out parish-wide corruption with no shame, and I openly opposed a ballot measure calling for the erection of a new parish courthouse, which would have costed taxpayers in the 28th District roughly two million dollars. These two actions did not sit well with the parish political establishment; however, countless voters I had met and talked to were firmly opposed to the measure.

I argued strongly that the millions of taxpayer dollars intended for the courthouse could be much better financed towards infrastructure, education, and community initiative programs for children, particularly after-school and summer programs. I opposed the erection of the new courthouse also on the grounds that it was set to be erected directly across the street from a school in the district, which could have posed a safety hazard for children in the event of a potential breakout by inmates. Furthermore, I felt that it would be far less expensive to the taxpayers to simply renovate the top floor of the current courthouse, which had gone unused for so many years. While this position was very unpopular in the eyes of the establishment class, it was welcomed with open arms by the everyday citizens of the district, and those were the individuals in which I sought to fight for each day as a legislator.

In the final weeks leading up to Election Day, I learned that I was doing very well in the polls. Deshotel led first in the polls, followed by me and Milligan, who was in third place. I was continuing to knock on more and more doors each day, speak at public events, and maintain a prominent presence on social media. I also conducted a small campaign rally in my hometown. By this time, a fourth candidate had entered the race. Ramondo Ramos was a Hispanic rancher and contractor who was relatively unknown and unpopular in some circles. Ramos held steady at fourth place in most polls.

There were some who were predicting the possibility of a run-off election between Deshotel and myself. While I never wanted to hold my hopes too high, I was cautiously optimistic in the expectation of a run-off. As October 12th, 2019 had finally approached, I was filled with a major source of positive energy. I spent the morning and afternoon at a fall festival in town and returned home just hours before the polls closed. An entire mass of individuals and supporters began reaching out to me on social media, informing me that I had their votes and that they were hoping I would come out on top.

As the polls were closing, I drove to the parish courthouse to listen as the results were coming in. While there were candidates in other races present, I was the only candidate from my race in attendance. Many of them had begun to leave as their returns were not looking very well. As the first set of returns began pouring in, I was in third place as Deshotel and Milligan were in first and second, respectively. I was feeling a bit worried, but the radio moderator reminded me that the present returns did not yet include certain districts I was predicted to do well in. After more and more returns came in, I advanced into second place behind Deshotel. However, it became quickly apparent that Deshotel would emerge as the winner, and the event of a runoff was highly unlikely. Deshotel achieved more than fifty percent of the entire vote, avoiding a predicted runoff between he and myself. He was also the first Republican legislator from the 28th District in many decades.

One of the factors that aided then-Representative-elect Deshotel's victory was the party transformation of local politics due to the overwhelming support among 28th District voters for then-President Trump. Upon learning that my numbers' path to victory was highly unlikely, I departed from the courthouse and returned home. During the drive home, I called Deshotel by phone and congratulated him on an honest, well-fought campaign and pledged my support in any required assistance to better the quality of life in the district we both love and call home. Many peaceful words were exchanged during the warm and heartfelt conversation. There was no bitterness or hard feelings to any extent. Even during the election cycle, no negative or nasty attacks took place among any of the four candidates vying for state representative.

The race ended with Deshotel as victor with over seven-thousand votes, me in 2nd place with over twenty-three hundred votes, Milligan in 3rd place with roughly twenty-one hundred votes, and Ramos with much less than a thousand votes. So many individuals, including family, friends, and supporters, were deeply proud of how well I worked, especially with little money and no legitimate campaign structure. In the eyes of many who were in my corner, twenty-three hundred votes were considered a massive achievement for being such a young and first-time candidate in a state legislature race. I was also encouraged to continue strongly in life and not give up on prospective future political endeavors that I may desire to explore. After a matter of weeks, I returned to teaching, made up for lost time with friends, and continued with life more strongly and blessed than ever before that time.

The First, but Wholeheartedly Not the Last

My run for state representative in the 28th District in Louisiana in 2019 remains one of the most critical endeavors I have ever undertaken so far. One question I have asked myself time and time again consists of the following: if I had to, would I do it all over again? The answer to this question is absolutely without a doubt. By a significant long shot, I do not regret all the work in which had to be done in obtaining legitimate name recognition as a candidate for state office. I do not regret overcoming a mass of obstacles amidst the most uncertain circumstances. I do not regret the long hours of walking in the scorching heat, burning and sweating like I had never done before. I will never take for granted the amazing people that I had the pleasure of meeting as well as the lasting connections that manifested as a result of spirited conversations. More than anything else, I do not regret coming up short on the final day of it all and responding to the outcome with humility, character, and decency, which is something that has become an admirable rarity in today's political climate.

The reason I do not regret the outcome of the election is that I know truly in my heart that I represented a cause much greater than my own desire to hold public office, and that the power of democracy will forever speak volumes when time demands it. I am not quite sure at this time when I may run for office again in the future or what office I will seek. However, when the hands of fate touch down on me and echo that call to service once more, I will proceed with that same boundless faith of character, integrity, honesty, and morality entrusted in me in 2019 by the hardworking, everyday citizens who define the 28th District. I will forever remember the many individuals I have served over the years through mentorship and community service.

I will recall the echoes of countless voices yearning for a heightened quality of human life. I will strive faithfully to re-assess certain policy measures that affect the lives of children and adolescents, strengthen the overall effectiveness of government so that it works for the people and the betterment of their lives, fight relentlessly on behalf of human rights and equal treatment under the law, and establish a coalition of citizens from all angles of the political spectrum to pursue an honest, meaningful conversation discussing the issues of poverty, systemic racism, climate change, gun violence, mental illness, and suicide. Just as I pledged to put the needs and best interests of people first during my initial run for public office, I would do just that once more when the almighty hands of fate decide to reach down and tell me once again when the time has come to proceed forward.

2

America Vs. America

"England and America are two separate countries separated by the same language."

--George Barnard Shaw

Under most circumstances, many of us would assume that it is humanly practical to strive for a long-term goal of unity in all collective acts of human behavior. Usually, it is morally instinctive for an individual to pursue behavioral actions that preserve and promote solidarity, peace, and stability. While there are indeed those who invoke havoc and division for the sole purpose of advancing a personal agenda, it is conventional for humanity to avoid conflict and discord due to the negative outcomes they bestow. Conflict and discord often apprehend the prospects for togetherness and teamwork, resulting in the potential desolation of partnerships.

If various nerves within certain individuals are pressed to a firm degree, potential outcomes may encompass both physical and mental destruction, violence, and death itself. This is the reason that some of us relent from discussing sensitive subject matters with certain loved ones or friends or acquaintances. We may omit certain words or are extra mindful of how we utter those words because we know how others may interpret them. Also, it is not unusual for many of us to avoid subject matters around certain times of the year such as Christmas or Thanksgiving or the anniversary of a tragically significant event. Again, these are commonplace standards on the part of humanity to simply maintain the peace by avoiding unpleasantries.

Much to humanity's dismay, there will always be those who would press firmly upon sensitive nerves in others and arouse controversial unpleasantries for the sole purpose of sowing conflict and discord. There are those who will deliberately pursue without conscience rhetoric that is highly offensive and historically insensitive. These individuals are often inconsiderate to the well-being of others and wholeheartedly oblivious to any reality beyond that of their own. The bar is raised when individuals in high positions of authority wield the power of their influence to stoke fear and division among the citizenries.

The critical questions we must ask ourselves consist of the following: why are certain individuals highly sensitive to various subject matters? Why do these subject matters invoke division and fear in the first place? What are the reasons that two different groups of humanity would respond or react so differently to the same subject matter or an event surrounding a certain subject matter? Is it politically and socially healthy to avoid discussing important matters just to avoid an uncomfortable emotional response? Are we acting truly in the greatest interests of unity and peace if we advocate for them both only for the mere sake of keeping things quiet? And what path must America pursue to resolve conflict and discord and division truly while achieving a credible foundation of lasting unity and peace? Providing credible insight into these questions will carry our nation a significant way.

The Roots of America's Division

The underlying roots of the division that exists in our country today has different tenets. Such tenets of division have been manifested in many variations: political, economic, racial, cultural, religious, gender, sexual orientation, social, etc. These layers in which America remains divided often run parallel to one's fundamental perspective of self, the world, and all the events for which take place in life itself. The first root of division lies in the initial state of difference; the second root of division lies in the perception of difference; the third root of division consists of the refusal to explore, understand, accept, and embrace that difference; the fourth and final root of division lies in discrimination, conflict, violence, war, death, and separation as the results of difference.

Our nation's division exist in terms of how we perceive one another on the surface and how we interpret forms of rhetoric and behavior. Our perceptions and interpretations of one another and different words and behavioral acts often dictate how we treat others. While the perceptions and interpretations of some are rooted in open-mindedness, optimism, and love, others have been manipulated in the toxic fumes of prejudgment, negativity, and hate. The power of perception and interpretation may harness either the power of drawing us closer to one another out of curiosity and compassion, crafting the foundation for collective growth, or it may harness deep-seated evil that may drive us farther apart out of callousness, ignorance, and fear. Furthermore, those who react with the latter to all that is perceived as unfamiliar and different from them do so because of the perceived threat to all that was previously known to be.

To great misfortune, there will always be those from all walks of life who respond to the new and the different with negativity. They will proceed in their personal lives as if they are superior to others. Some will proceed as far as to establish a precedent for public life that deems certain ways and aspects of life as inferior to theirs. Rather than attempt to explore what is new and different for clarity and greater understanding, some individuals will rely on narrow-minded, falsely narrated images to with whom and what they have never come into true contact. These images, often based on historical standards of perfection, are crafted by mainstream media as well as studies of history. Individuals of a certain race or ethnicity or way of life who have lived and grown up in an area that is predominant to their kind are vulnerable to baseless perceptions of life because they have yet to understand and experience humanity from a broader, more diverse perspective.

Consistent callousness, fear, and negativity in the hearts of some stand to only destroy us all by blinding us to what is decent and good, hindering prospects for collective growth and progress. This often causes some to overlook the fact that we are all human and crafted perfectly in the eyes of God. Misguided perceptions and interpretations cause us to not only dismiss a vast degree of all that we *have* in common but negate the fact that we as human beings are capable of having *anything* in common at all. This is followed by efforts to establish opposing standards, under the false pretenses of purity and safety, in which to dictate our lives. These shallow, opposing standards exist as the foundation of discriminatory laws in addition to culturally dominant as well as morally superior attitudes.

Historically, this foundation has always been followed by civil unrest, acts of war and violence, the loss of human life, and separation. This has been carried out in the United States countless times in pertaining to injustices against people of color, women, and the LGBTQIAP community. This can be seen carried out also in Indonesia as its government has imposed a moralist view on its people by regulating personal and sexual relations between private citizens. This specific point will be discussed much more in depth in the following chapter.

You may recall the title of this chapter *America Vs. America*. Let us store emphasis for a moment on the first half of the title. It is no doubt that everyone knows America, sometimes referred to as the United States, to exist as a country. Most of us have known this country to be the freest, most prosperous society since the origin of human civilization. The world knows this country we call America, the *United States* of America, to be the most diverse and inclusive and culturally rich society to ever exist. All of us, black and white, young and old, gay and straight, cisgender and transgender, religious and non-religious, and all for which lies in between with no one of any kind to be singled out, equally define America's rich bastion of humanity. The everyday people of our country, teachers and students, cops and firefighters, entrepreneurs and doctors, pastors and churchgoers, and the cashiers and fast-food workers making only minimum wage, create unseen riches that extend throughout an entire population.

Generations have long known America to be a significant source of light and opportunity to all those who yearn for a better future. Americans from all ends of the political spectrum, Democrats and Republicans, liberals and conservatives, and independents and libertarians, all share a longstanding vision for the path we must choose in continuing the two-hundred, forty-seven-year journey our Founders began in 1776. No single group of citizens in this country holds any monopoly on the basic human values of life, pain and suffering, patriotism, or solutions to the problems afflicting humanity each day. What affects one directly affects all others indirectly. All of us in the United States of America are inextricably bound to the roots of a single shaped destiny, and we must re-begin the work of cementing this reality into fate without cause for reverse.

If you were to refer to the title of this chapter, you would see that the second half of the title is the exact same the first half. One may inquire for the reason as to why both parts are the same thing. There are two reasons for the repeat. The first reason is that all of us in America are the same indeed! However, as stated earlier, there are some in this country who do not believe in our shared values nor our shared destiny as a people. There are many who believe that some of us in this country hold societal superiority to others in many aspects. There are some who hold an alarming degree of political righteousness that is beyond quick to dismiss all that is beyond a familiar reality, and this is the second reason that the chapter is entitled the way that it is. Not only does America's greatest adversary lies within, but her greatest present adversary is also her own self!

The Unwarranted Conversation

Earlier on in the chapter, there are a set of questions concerning the avoidance of conflict, discord, and division amid sensitive subject matters. I asked why some of us avoid certain topics and for the possible reasons those topics stir controversy; I inquired for the possible reasons certain groups respond so differently to the same thing; I asked the reader to consider if it is healthy and productive in the long-term to promote togetherness for the mere sake of remaining peaceful and calm. Also, I inquired for the path that must be pursued to change course for the better.

Firstly, allow me to state very succinctly: avoiding the discussion of a subject matter because of the nerve it may shake and the controversy it may manifest is destructive in the long-term.

Secondly, avoiding the discussion of various subject matters only allows deep-seated sensitivity to grow on steroids, making the surface issue significantly more difficult to resolve in its entirety. Thirdly, the so-called unity and peace that we often seek to maintain by dismissing longstanding sensitive issues will only dissolve over time as tension becomes worse. Fourthly and final, dismantling division, conflict, discord, and all the negative consequences that follow along will begin with an honest, optimism-based, and long-term conversation concerning all the issues for which bestows sensitivity, discomfort, and offense. Coming together must extend beyond a physical togetherness and consist of a foundation that exists in understanding, compassion, love, empathy, and acceptance of truth without bias of any kind.

All citizens in the United States of America must be willing to step beyond the mantrum walls of their own reality. We as Americans must realize that each of us are the same at heart not only as humans but because of the ideals that define our nation's greatness in history and the world. We are the same not only because we bleed the same color or because of the basic abilities and common attributes of the human body or because someday all of us will die but because we seek what is good and pure and reject what bestows harm and injustice. Our different outwardly responses to the issues plaguing our country are only a mere reflection of the same emotional responses in our hearts.

What we perceive to appear different from our opposite realities must not cause either of us to believe that we are different at the core. Our perception of difference must not blind us to a false reality where desolation and suffering are inevitable. To truly solve our division and achieve lasting unity, we must be willing to open ourselves individually and collectively to the sensitive issues that bring discomfort and displeasure in discussing due to their historical realities. This will allow us to reverse a longstanding invisible stalemate built in deep-seated tension, hidden resentment towards others, and lasting frustration with a lack of progress.

The questions going forward consists of the following: what group of citizens is unwilling to pursue the much-needed conversations required for progress? What consists of the issues certain individuals refuse to acknowledge and discuss? Before I seek to answer this question, I will acknowledge that many from this group may proclaim that it will contradict the entire argument that I am making concerning our nation's state of division. However, I would counter-respond by proclaiming that we must know who is responsible for our division and hold them accountable if we intend to overcome it. Furthermore, our nation can never achieve true and lasting unity while some of us are unashamedly hellbent on the opposite. The group that is most responsible for the contemporary division taking place in America consists of radical far right MAGA Republicans. All of us know well that the thinking pattern of the MAGA far right stems from an outdated, warn out method of thinking that is anathema to not only the vision of our Framers but the current reality of today.

The Trump-MAGA cult, also known as the radical far right, is nothing like anything we as Americans have seen for quite some time. Not only does the Trump-MAGA cult quest stand in anathema to the vision of our Founding Fathers, but it also denounces all that opposes its ideology. Anyone and any idea that opposes the absolute power quest of Donald Trump is portrayed as the greatest enemy to America; however, any person with common sense and a true love for this country knows that the greatest threat to American greatness is Donald Trump and his allies. Our nation witnessed the countless times when former President Trump and his allies had declared enemies out of all those who opposed them. Let us never forget the times when so many were told to "go back from where they came" when they acknowledged the problems that exist because of Trump-MAGA. Let us remember the countless personal insults and threats of violence put forth by Trump-MAGA in the effort to destroy those who opposed the movement.

Let us never forget or downplay the dangerous accusation concerning the 2020 presidential election for which caused so much damage and havoc to the lives of so many Americans and that has yet to proven beyond a reasonable doubt. The Trump-MAGA cult sees anything or anyone who opposes its movement as inferior, and the movement itself is the most divisive and toxic element of political activism our country has ever witnessed. It sees an America that speaks two languages, only because most of us would never dare to speak the un-American language of Trump-MAGA.

Trump-MAGA cult perspectives concerning America's future is beyond dangerous and stands to upend countless lives if it continues its divisive tirade. This argument does not contradict the greater argument concerning unity because the masterminds and perpetrators have made it clear that they do not believe in unity as well as the vision of our Founders. This was clear when former President Trump encouraged his supporters on January 6th to "fight like hell." It was clear when Rudy Giuliani declared "trial by combat" at the same rally on January 6th. How about when disgraced Congressperson Majorie Taylor Greene proclaimed that if rioters would have been armed with guns and "had have won" if she and former Trump advisor Steve Bannon had overseen the January 6th insurrection? What about when the president of the New York Young Republican

Club, Gavin Wax, declared that the following "We want to cross the Rubicon. We want total war. We must be prepared to do battle in every arena. In the media. In the courtroom. At the ballot box. And in the streets," NYYRC president Gavin Wax declared to a room full of supporters at 583 Park Ave., an event venue on New York's Upper East Side. Not to mention, the same white supremacists at the Charlottesville riot declaring that "Jews would not place us" are part of the Trump-MAGA cult. Trump-MAGA has declared war on its own country! It does not possess that moral instinctive to promote unity and solidarity due to its own personal agenda. Instead of embracing America's values and seeking out the good in others as fellow humans, it has chosen to invoke havoc, hate-filled rhetoric, and violent extremism time and time again.

What makes this situation so unfortunate is that the Trump-MAGA cult consists of approximately half of our country's entire population. This means that nearly half of the country is secretly sensitive to the critical issues of our country's future. Pertaining to various issues concerning race, human rights, poverty, gun violence, and climate change, MAGA Republicans appear so uninterested that they are not even willing to bring sensible ideas to the table in moving our entire country forward. The reality consists of the irony of deep sensitivity due to the historical and cultural responsibility in solving these issues. This is the reason that the required conversations are unwarranted.

Trump-MAGA is so hellbent on not participating in as well as dismissing conversations concerning certain issues that it is difficult to forge national consensus concerning a way forward. The radical far right is an un-American movement that does not even speak on behalf the traditional conservative movement nor the establishment Republican Party in the United States. For much of our history, Americans from all political spectrums have stood firm for our nation's identity when time demanded it. Each time they did came with great sacrifice and brought about enormous progress.

So, the path going forward is very simple: those who subscribe wholeheartedly to the Trump-MAGA cult can accept responsibility for the great damage it has caused to American democracy over the past few years. It can accept the reality that Donald Trump is interested solely in his own quest for power and could not care any less for the people that he manipulates or destroys in fulfilling his political quests. Finally, it can finally stop the madness and join with the rest of us.

The final choice for Trump-MAGA is to either join hands with the rest of America to move our country forward or simply step aside and stop blocking the much-needed progress we need for a future that will lift us all. Either get on board or get out of the way. While the rest of us should always stand for unity and solidarity, we must do so if it is based on a solid and true foundation. It begins with holding Trump-MAGA accountable fully, and doing so must take place at the polls, the peaceful protest march, or in the courts. Afterwards, we can finally move America forward.

3

The Human Rights Debate and Why It Is More Vital Than Ever Before

"Human rights are not a privilege conferred by government. They are every human being's entitlement by virtue of their humanity."

--Mother Theresa

As of the year 2021, the population of the world had reached an astounding 7.9 billion. By that same year, the United States population had reached an estimated 331.9 million. Both numbers can be quite underestimated if they are interpreted on paper alone. However, each one consists of a massive quantity. What helps me to truly fathom numbers with great depths of value is to imagine a football field covered entirely with human beings lying down. It would take approximately 54,000 human beings to completely cover a typical American football field. This means it would take 6,146 American football fields to hold every American at the current national population; it would require 146,296 American football fields to hold every citizen of the entire world at its current population. Witnessing this with the naked eye would be phenomenally mind blowing.

Fifty-four thousand is substantially less than 331.9 million as well as a whopping 7.9 billion. The greatest significance of these population numbers lies in the fact that they are not referring to physical objects for which possess no ability to feel or move according to their own free will. The significance lies in knowing that they are referring to people. This means that there are over 7.9 billion individual minds, souls, and perspectives of life in the world, while 331.9 million of those exist in the United States alone. Each of these humans has personal feelings, customs, and loved ones. Each one of them has blood flowing throughout their veins. Furthermore, each individual desires to be treated a certain way by others.

The next great significance of the large populations is that they stand to continue increasing substantially over the course of humanity's existence. The UN projects the world's population to increase to 9.7 billion by the year 2050. Furthermore, it projects the population to increase to 10.4 billion individuals by the year 2100. The world is growing rapidly consistently; as a result, the demands of humankind and methods of fulfilling those demands will forever grow and transform. Meeting the demands of humanity often bestow debate upon many concerning the methods of meeting those demands.

Most of humanity's demands for survival are centered upon basic access to healthy food, clean water, shelter, and medical care; while we often disagree with one another concerning how to increase the quality of access to a basic standard of living, the mere fact of disagreement is not a cause for sounding alarms. What causes alarms to sound as loud as they could ever be is when some of us not only assert mere disagreement but pursue physical and administrative action against the greatest demand of human civilization: the basic human right to simply exist and be treated with basic dignity and respect in every aspect of human life.

Every human being on the face of the Earth has been bestowed the basic human right by almighty God to function normally in everyday society without being denied fully adequate and equal access to a basic standard of living. No human should ever be subjugated to discrimination of any kind or physical assault or death simply because others may be uncomfortable or offended by how they look or how they live. Furthermore, no human should ever be denied employment, healthcare, housing, access to quality education, and a sense of safety due to someone's personal views or difference of opinion.

The only kind of people who would be offended by the previous paragraph consists of those who simply do not believe that we are all equal in the eyes of God, and they will apply every method at their disposal, even stooping so low by manipulating the love of Jesus Christ, to justify their own sense of superiority as well as the mistreatment of those they deem inferior. They will project their own hate onto God as if He Himself would condone injustice or the physical destruction or wrongful death of others.

Rather than apply the unconditional love of Christ to uplift all the children of God without favoritism, they will manipulate that love to condemn and destroy all who is simply different from who they are. All of those who do agree that we are all worthy of being respected and that the life of no person deserves to be attacked and discriminated against simply because of who they are would have no problems performing all actions deemed necessary and beyond to defeat every threat to the first and most basic human right of every child of God, which is to exist.

The Greatest Fundamental Task of Our Time

I have always been adamantly passionate about political activism since high school. Every single issue affecting the lives of the American people arouses my greatest interest and concern. The sole issue of human rights, however, has always attracted my greatest discernment. The basic human right to simply exist without experiencing physical and verbal harassment or unequal treatment under the law is the single most important life or death issue in America today. It is a grave shame, first and foremost, that this must even be a concern among us.

Treating each person with the greatest respect and decency is simply common sense. Most of us as human beings would assume that all individuals would fulfill this standard automatically without debate. The reason that we cannot is because of the ancient idea among some which consist of the following: the belief that one kind is superior to all others and anything that is different from their kind is inferior. As a result of this toxic conviction, so many individuals from all over the world have suffered tremendously. Many of these individuals have died.

During the era of Reconstruction, over two-thousand African Americans were lynched. Many more endured constant discriminations and were simply mistreated by the worst methods possible. Many blacks were beaten in the streets, raped, spat on, and afforded the worst standard of living imaginable. They also endured unimaginable mental health conditions because of this profound belittlement towards their ancestors as well as themselves directly.

All those who utter the rhetoric saying that some of us need to forget about the past often fail to remember that the mistreatment of people of color that began hundreds of years ago is a direct cause of the unfair and unjust socio-economic and cultural conditions that exist today. The disproportionalities among people of color that exist in economic and educational opportunities as well as basic access to adequate healthcare and fair housing in contrast to non-people of color are a direct result of the physical bondages of slavery as well as the horrors of the Jim-Crow era.

Radical far right extremists will often state that the reason racism continues to exist is because some of us continue to "complain about the past." If these same individuals would choose to do their research and stop proceeding off ignorant and ill-informed convictions, they would realize that being honest about the reality and the history of race and discussing these issues in great detail would dissolve any need to discuss the issue of race in the absolute beginning.

Due to the mere thought that a single individual felt as if he was superior to all that was different from him and as if they are inferior, countless human beings have lost their lives and continue to do so. Once again, thousands of people of color and whites together have died, over six million Jews were slaughtered, many women have been battered, raped, and lost their lives, and countless citizens of the LGBTQIAP community have suffered massive humiliation as well as injustice and have been murdered in the form of hate crimes.

The issue of human rights and equal treatment under the law is extremely personal to me. First and foremost, it is a matter of profound common sense and a greater sense of right from wrong. As someone who strives each day as a Christian and a human being to become more like Christ and better practice right from wrong because no one is perfect, I am highly offended when some develop excuses to treat others poorly only because they are different. Secondly, I have many relatives and close friends who do not fulfill the white straight cisgender male standards, and I would never want to see them hurt or possibly lose their lives because of how they look or how they live. Thirdly, the notion that all those who assert that they love those who are different from them but are OK with those who are in fact different being treated poorly is no longer justifiable nor acceptable.

Those who develop all possible excuses to discriminate against or chastise those who are different usually attempt to justify their assertions with religious or biblical scriptures pertaining to the condemnation of light with darkness, the second-class treatment of women, and the destruction of LGBTQIAP community. President Lincoln once stated the following very eloquently: "Whenever I hear anyone arguing for slavery, I feel a strong impulse to see it tried on him personally." To all the racists, the bigots, the xenophobes, the misogynists, the homophobes, and the transphobes, how would they feel if the same oppression they may simply wish upon or even pursue against those are different from them was applied to their lives? How would they feel if someone or a group of individuals sought to curtail their basic human right to exist and their access to a basic standard of living?

If we as a country are to resolve the issue of and overcome the sin of injustice, we all need to be honest with ourselves and take the issue into full perspective. We need to stop evading the issue as it is due to personal void or how uncomfortable it be while discussing it. As of 2016, there has been a massive effort to return the fundamental way of life in the United States to the former white straight cisgender male socio-economic and cultural standards of the past. This is evident in the countless discriminatory laws that have been passed in many states as well as the current national mood among MAGA radical far right Republicans.

Whether it be the laws and statutes passed in Florida attacking and belittling citizens of the LGBTQIAP community or banning African American college courses, those passed in Georgia seeking to diminish the right to vote, the overturning of Roe v. Wade at the national level, or the effort to make Texas its own country, they are all efforts to reverse the half of century accomplishments on behalf of greater equity under the law. The blatant attack on our basic human right to exist and function normally in everyday society should be viewed as unfathomable no longer because the fact of the matter is that is taking place before our very own eyes in real time. What is happening before us today is the most dangerous and unprecedented attack on human rights in the United States since the height of the

Twentieth Century. Drastic consequences will follow if we do not reverse course immediately.

Let me make this assertion extremely clear. This is not an attack on any particular race, gender, sexual orientation, gender identity, or ethnicity. This is also not an attack on the American people overall. This is not intended to racially bash or condemn every single non-person of color. None of this, however, should negate the hard evidence that people of color in this country have endured and continue to endure a grave reality that non-people of color have never had to endure on a largely disproportionate scale simply because of the color of their skin. This reality should serve only as an urgent reminder that we have much more work to do in America. In acknowledging the white straight cisgender male norms of the past, it is strictly referring to an ideology that is transferred into human practice.

This is not a specific attack on individuals who merely happen to be white, straight, cisgender, and male, and I, personally, do not speak for anyone who harbors secret animosities or prejudices for those who happen to be white, straight, cisgender, and male. At the same time, no individual should ever proceed to misguided conclusions when one calls out practices based on a thought pattern that is responsible for centuries of generational torture. The fact that so many in one of our mainstream political parties would play politics with such a complicated and life-threatening issue only demonstrates the disappointing lack of urgency they feel towards justice and equality for all.

It is hypocritical for most of them to cry injustice when the FBI raided former President Trump's home at Mar-a-Lago and carry forward with physical and verbal attacks on law enforcement when officials sought to contain insurrectionists from breaching the Capitol on January 6th but refuse to address decades of injustice, hate crimes, and police brutality on superficial grounds, only to dismiss those claims or even state that incidents of police brutality, injustice, and hate crimes are people's own fault.

It is important for all of us to remember that there are countless non-people of color who would sacrifice their lives and state more clearly and better than I ever could that there is an issue of systemic injustice in America that has a direct but negative and disproportionate impact on people of color, women of all backgrounds, and those who identify as gay, lesbian, bisexual, or transgender. There are also countless non-people of color who have realized and acknowledged the dangerously increasing re-conformity to profound intolerance since the rise of the Trump-MAGA movement in 2016 as well as the attempt to reverse all that our nation has accomplished since the height of the civil rights movement during the 1960s.

To hold deep-seated bitterness or hatred towards non-people of color or America in general would be counterproductive in all efforts to protect equal rights and just as dangerous as the original hatred that has toppled the lives of far too many. Our efforts to finally put an end to the longstanding stalemate of racial inequality in this country should be centered upon unwavering optimism and greater trust in one another as Americans as well as the children of almighty God. The greatest path forward is to escape denial of an ideology-turned-practice that not only has destroyed the lives of so many but stands to lead our nation to a second civil war. A second civil war is brewing, and we need to take a difference stance from what we have been doing for so long if we wish to prevent the potential destruction of our country and loss of countless lives in the future.

My Problem with Republicans Who Happen to be African American

I am a firm believer in a diversity of thinking. A variety of ideas concerning the issues to increase the quality of human life requires different ranges of thinking. Achieving that greater quality of life is impossible without a diversity of ideas. I also do not assume negatively of African Americans who feel that aligning with the Republican Party and a conservative method of thinking is a better way of life for people of color. I have never assumed negatively of those who believe and think differently from me. The initial different method of thinking is not the problem. My problem, however, is the refusal to acknowledge the unfortunate historical and socioeconomic and cultural reality of race in the United States.

I have a problem when people like Candace Owens assert that individuals such as George Floyd are savages and when Owens herself says that she is OK with discrimination. I have a problem when people like Hershel Walker parades before the most conservative individuals there are, making a mockery of the issues that are unique to people of color. I have a problem when the first African American Lieutenant Governor of North Carolina says that people like my best friend, who is a person of color, that is also a trans man is filth. I have a problem when the first Republican Chairman of color from the state of Texas, Lieutenant Colonel, Allen West, threw a tantrum on social media when his wife was pulled over in her car by the police for allegedly operating behind the wheel intoxicated with their granddaughter in the back seat but had nothing to say when George Floyd and Breonna Taylor and Jacob Blake and Tyre Nichols were murdered unlawfully by law enforcement. I have a problem when many Republicans who happen to be African American choose to betray other people of color by degrading them consistently and choosing to support public policies that only weaken access within the black community to a greater standard of living and make working-class African Americans much worse off.

As stated before, there lies nothing negative in being a conservative or a member of the Republican Party. Anyone is capable of being able to stand boldly and proudly and proclaim that the mistreatment of others due simply to how they look and how they live is profoundly wrong. Any conservative can choose to support policies that lift us all rather than a selected few. The fact alone that so many cannot take this bold but simple position for personally motivated reasons is the greatest motivation for the remainder to us to perform all that is necessary to reverse the state of injustice. No individual deserves to lose their mother or father, sister or brother, aunt or uncle or cousin, or best friend simple because a certain person feels they are superior to them.

No individual should ever have the right to degrade or discriminate against any other person because they simply feel it is OK. Those who are people of color have direct and personal contact with systemic injustice simply because they are people of color. The fact that they would deny it is because are trying to appease the racist factions of their political party or simply trying to escape the unfortunate reality of injustice. Maybe they need to take lessons from the first African American

Secretary of State, General Colin Powell, an individual who garnered the greatest admiration and respect from Americans of all races and in both political parties. While he would eventually become an Independent over a year before his passing, he was never afraid and never relented in standing for what he knew in his heart to be true and hold his party accountable when they failed to live up to the ideals of our greater selves.

Colin Powell did not allow something as insignificant as a party label to prevent him from addressing the challenges and negative stigmas plaguing the black community. He never once sought to escape the sick reality of racism by pretending as if it does not exist. Powell never gaslighted fellow African Americans for calling it out not nor did he seek to appease white supremacy just to make himself look good from the extreme element of his party.

People like Candace Owens, Larry Elder, Sage Steele, Allen West, Herschel Walker, the Lieutenant Governor Mark Robinson of North Carolina, Jesse Lee Peterson, and so many more should apologize wholeheartedly to all the current citizens of this country who they have called slaves and how individuals need to get off the plantations. Individuals such as these will constantly lecture the African American community about hard work, responsibility, and self-excellence. The fact of the matter is this: these values transcend both race and political ideology. Striving diligently for greatness in life is something we all embrace, and I have taught this principle to young people for years now. However, the act of doing so will not erase the reality of systemic racism in this country.

No matter how well a person of color may speak, dress, or behave, it will not stop that person from possibly being pulled over while driving a fancy car in a predominantly white neighborhood. None of these things will eliminate all prospects for various incidents of discrimination. Leading an upstanding life will not escape the wrath of police brutality. Overall, these things will unfortunately not omit a person of color from experiencing the harsh reality of racial injustice for which still lingers today in various aspects. What will begin the reversal of the harsh reality of racism in America today is a complete analysis of public policy; it will progress firmly when individuals of every kind begin to educate themselves fully on every reality of life beyond that of their own; it will end when lawmakers at every level of leadership stop making the same excuses again and again to not uproot hundreds of years of practices based on deep-seated racial superiority that has been passed down from generation to generation.

The time has come for African American culture to stop being perceived as a crime. African Americans should be at full liberty, like all others, to express themselves in terms of hairstyle, personal attire, and language/dialect without being perceived to be a criminal. Every person should have the freedom to be their self without being degraded by others as a human being altogether. Also, the time has come to stop referring to African Americans as victims for calling out and denouncing institutional bias and associating people of color with identity politics simply because they choose to not align with a political movement that does not respect and honor their mere existence. For many Republicans of color or anyone else to scrutinize people of color as well as our ancestors is an absolute shame.

It would be accurate to state that constant scrutiny and condemnation from Republicans who happen to be black would account for the fact that between eighty and ninety percent of African Americans have an overwhelmingly negative perspective of them as well as the Republican Party altogether. The consistent scrutiny towards blacks and the refusal to offer viable solutions to longstanding issues plaguing the black community may account for why it is seen as an act of betrayal among people of color for an African American to align with the radical far right. All those African American conservatives who have put down the community repeatedly should apologize to both their ancestors and individuals such as Martin Luther King, Jr., Rosa Parks, and Medgar Evers as well as all those whom they have disgraced just to fulfill the wishes of the very idea that has caused so much destruction and death.

People of color have endured the sin of racism long before our country had been established, and for anyone to downplay the struggles that so many endure today and what many who are still alive can recall vividly is beyond unfortunate and unfair. In moving forward, we must initiate a national conversation concerning the reality of race in America and develop a step-by-step vision in abolishing systemically biased practices, eliminating economic and educational disproportionalities, enacting meaningful police reform at the national level, and empowering all people of color to be active consistent in our democracy.

Toxic Masculinity

The great ChimamandaNgoziAdichie has stated the following: "But by far the worst thing we do to males — by making them feel they must be hard is that we leave them with very fragile egos. The harder a man feels compelled to be, the weaker his ego is." Let us analyze the reality beneath this quote. Toxic masculinity, first and foremost, is a derivative of the larger white supremacy tent. Since the beginning of time, the belief that men should portray this ruffian, tough guy persona has served as a fundamental conventional standard.

The idea that a man should always dominate all that is around him has been ingrained in our minds since birth. In other terms, relating to the quote, a man must be "hard" for him to be perceived in accordance with the traditional standards of how men are supposed to behave. This hardness is based on a narcissistic, grandiose outlook of the world that basically tells a man and everyone else considering unfortunate situations to simply "get over it" or "be a man." Basic common-sense things such as crying out for assistance when needed or expressing deep-seated emotions have become categorized as strict feminine-like traits.

According to current conventional wisdom, all men are expected to talk "hard," walk "hard," dress "hard,", and demonstrate various kinds of "hard" responses in certain situations. Examples of those responses include reacting with mere force or even violence in confrontational situations, refusing to apply logic and conscience in tempting situations, and concealing emotions under most circumstances. Men are also expected, unfortunately, to always exert authority and ruthless control when there are women involved, whether it be in the home or in a position of political power. Men are expected and encouraged to sleep with as many women as possible and receive great praise for it, while a woman will be chastised and belittled for merely exhibiting the slightest hint of doing the same thing!

If a man does not adhere to these long-time, conventional standards, he will be perceived as weak or "soft" by individuals of all genders. If he behaves like a gentleman, he will likely be perceived to be a pushover. Furthermore, in the event of a man not adhering to conventional toxic masculinity, he will also be referred to as gay, as if the state of being gay is a negative thing. Again, this is a deeply unfortunate stigma that has existed since the beginning of the time and still exists today. This is an additional example of being mistreated and chastised for being different.

As a result of these conventional toxic masculine standards, so many individuals have suffered, continue to suffer, and others simply lose out on various opportunities to get ahead in life. Women have had to fight for generations just to receive the right to vote, equal pay for doing the same work as men, and an equal seat at the table in just about every aspect of human life. While women have achieved sizable progress in obtaining equal access to various opportunities, most women are still forced to endure scrutiny, disrespect, sexual harassment, and discrimination in just about every industry there is. As of the year 2017, over four in ten women have reported gender discrimination in the workplace. Let us not neglect to mention the countless instances of sexual and physical assault that women often endure not only on the job but in so many other places.

An aspect of the current conventional wisdom consists of the notion that women exist for the sole purpose of pleasing men, which is based solely on an old-time, hormonal, and narrowly minded motivation. This may greatly explain why many men fail to acknowledge that no means no and proceed with unwanted sexual advances on a woman, even after she has made it abundantly clear that she is not interested in pursuing the act. This also explains the existence of human sex trafficking against women and female adolescents.

Toxic masculinity increases incidents of rape and domestic violence because the man often feels that the woman has a duty to fulfill him sexually and obey him in all other aspects. To translate, toxic masculinity asserts that a woman is seen as good only in the "kitchen and the bedroom." This would explain why Roe v. Wade was overturned after so many decades, which will have a detrimental effect on the health and overall well-being of women across the United States. This also explains why there are laws in multiple states across the nation for which allow rapists to sue their victims for parental rights if the victim became pregnant as a result of the rape. This may be one of the most absurd and worse administrative attacks against women in this country to have ever taken place. It has been proven that women who lack access to basic reproductive health options are likely to endure a great decline in mental health in contrast to those who do have access, possibly being pushed to the brink of suicide.

Among those who have suffered and continue to suffer greatly because of toxic masculinity are those who identify as part of the LGBTQIAP community. All instances of human rights' abuse angers me to the absolute fullest; however, consistent attacks on gays, lesbians, bisexuals, and transgender men and women anger me uniquely because they are often justified by being separated from attacks towards African Americans and cisgender women. The assertion is that individuals do not get to choose their skin color or biological gender at birth but can, in fact, choose to their gender identity or sexual orientation. Whether one can choose to be gay or trans is irrelevant, and I would respond with the following: the bottom line in any aspect of human rights' abuse is inferiority. One who feels deeply as if all who are different from him is inferior to him do not care if those who are different chose to be who they are or if they consist of a certain way by nature.

A white supremacist would not demonstrate the slightest bit of sympathy if a person of color chose to be that way. If someone could choose their own skin color, that would have been more of a reason for a white supremacist to put a gun to an African American's head and tell them to make their self white or they will be killed or continue to be treated poorly. Just as those who demonstrate disdain and hatred for those who are gay, lesbian, or transgender would not feel any different if individuals were that way by nature. Gays, lesbians, bisexuals, and trans men and trans women would still endure grave injustice as well as unjustifiable hate crimes from the very people who have declared them to be inferior to their so-called counterparts.

Let us consider those who are black but also happen to be gay or transgender or both. Not only does someone in this predicament must endure the longstanding tragedy of racism, but they must also face the pain of homophobia and transphobia. The individual will be seen by some as an even greater abomination, and the stigma in which they will endure based on three completely shallow premises will be a hundred times worse than just one of those premises alone. There are over 1.2 million African Americans who identify as LGBTQIAP in some form. African Americans who identify as gay or transgender experience poverty, economic hardship, and hunger at greater levels than non-LGBTQIAP African Americans.

Blacks who identify as gay or trans are much more susceptible to both mental and physical health disparities as well as a lack of access to healthcare, and over eighty-two percent of the group reports to experiencing everyday discrimination. Furthermore, an overwhelming majority of African American LGBTQIAP individuals have reported experiences with threats of violence, physical and sexual abuse, and verbal insults in public. These statistics come from the UCLA Williams Institute. These statistics only prove that the argument of "by nature or by choice" is only more of a failed justification attempt on the part of those who have declared superiority to defend their disdain for those who are different from them. Also, this talking point is just another disgraceful example of selective equality, which is only just more oppression against certain marginalized groups.

I am sure there are many individuals who may be familiar with the name Barbara Jordan. In 1966, during the height of the civil rights movement, Barbara Jordan became the first African American woman to serve as a state senator in Texas as well as the first African American overall to serve in this position since 1883 at the time. She was the first woman of color to serve as governor of a state, the first woman to represent the state of Texas in Congress, and the first African American woman from a Southern state to serve in Congress.

Jordan's momentous legacy moves the hearts of many, but what many of us do not know is that she also identified as lesbian. Her lifelong partner was a white woman named Nancy Earl, who would eventually become Jordan's caretaker as Jordan's health began to decline. So, not only did Barbara Jordan make history as an African American and a woman in many aspects, but she was also the first woman who identified as LGBTQIAP to serve in Congress.

In the eyes of the shallow, Jordan's identity consisted of three attributes that would assign her to the bottom of the food chain automatically: she was black, she was a woman, and she was gay. By these three standards alone, the shallow saw her as an abomination who was destined only for the abyss. In the eyes of reality, Barbara Jordan was a beautiful child of God who fulfilled her God-given greatness with all odds against her. She was a profound inspiration who overcame massive obstacles during a time when injustice in America had reached its climax. She paved the way for so many who came after her time. More important than anything else, Barbara Jordan was human. She was a person and a citizen.

Jordan bled the same red blood that flows throughout the veins of us all. Not only did she not allow the evil of the shallow to diminish her success, but she also refused to allow that evil to break her spirit. She did not embrace the negative stigma bestowed upon her kind as her own view of self, and this is why I admire and respect Barbara Jordan. To separate bad apples that fall from the same tree is relatively pointless because it is merely a diversion from destroying the root from which all the bad apples derived to begin with.

Extreme far right special interest group, Council of Conservative Citizens, that referred once to people of color as "genetically inferior" referred also to Jews as "power brokers" and to gays as "perverted sodomites." The same white supremacist group, endorsed by radical right-wing journalist, Ann Coulter, opposes racial integration and interracial marriage. The plight of race, sexual orientation, and gender identity should never be separated; all of us are in this together. The only way to get out of it is by getting out together and stop trying to pick and choose who is more worthy in the eyes of God and which citizens are worthy of being respected as human beings because we all are!

Those who are racist are usually misogynistic, homophobic, and transphobic as well. Again, it is all part of the greater package of inferiority. I have blood relatives who identify as gay as well as very close friends who identify as gay, lesbian, bisexual, and transgender; I think of them directly and am deeply offended when individuals seek to verbally belittle or enact laws that target the LGBTQIAP community. Once again, the foundation is inferiority towards all those who are not white, straight, cisgender, and male. Furthermore, this country is based on the idea that all citizens are free and able to dictate the course of their own fate by designation of the Declaration of Independence and the Constitution. There is no logical or moral justification for the mistreatment of not only gay and transgender individuals but all Americans. All those who seek to justify the mistreatment of others on any premise is part of the problem in this country.

Again, so many individuals, including men themselves, have endured great pain and will continue to do so because of hardcore toxic masculine standards. The Pan American Health Organization forecasts that 1 in 5 men will not reach the age of 50, and it is related greatly to toxic masculinity. These standards result sometimes in homicide because of what I referred to earlier as the "tough guy" mentality that compromises the ability to apply logic and moral conscience in situations involving conflict, or simply because he may just feel the desire to hurt others just to prove a point to the world.

Suicide, alcoholism, and drug addiction, all of which are often the result of a decline in mental health, consist of deaths in men relating to toxic masculinity. Furthermore, concerning women, approximately thirty percent of women in the United States have experienced rape, physical violence, and stalking. Almost fifteen percent of women have experienced traumatic physical injuries because of the three things just listed.

Almost eighty percent of women experienced their first rape before the age of twenty-five.

As of 2021, almost sixty individuals who identify as transgender or gender non-conforming have lost their lives at the hands of gun violence. Let us not neglect to recall the recent mass shooting during a drag show at a gay nightclub in Colorado Springs where five individuals were brutally gunned down. This may be a low number, but each one represents a human being with families and friends who now are forced to live without them only because another individual saw them as inferior. There have been many more lives lost, brutalized, and mocked due to the view that men are supposed to adhere to certain standards that are toxic to not only themselves but all others, and the only reason any man or any person would seek to control others is because they have little to no control over themselves.

Overcoming the Greatest Domestic Threat of Our Time Once and For All

As stated earlier on and in my previous book *One Nation Under Trump*, there is a more than dangerous trend taking place in the United States concerning human rights. While countless states across America have enacted laws curtailing voting rights, restricting women's reproductive health options, and blatantly attacking the personal rights of the LGBTQIAP community, the movement may soon become a national effort. Former President Trump just proposed to abolish gender-affirming care for minors. He pledged, if elected in 2024, to also prohibit any federal agency from working to "promote the concept of sex and gender transition at any age." He already proved his disdain for trans men and trans women during his first and only term in the White House. One of former President Trump's first actions upon becoming our Commander in Chief was rolling back federal civil rights protections in terms of housing, employment, and law enforcement. He also instituted a ban on trans men and trans women from serving our country in our proud military, which was lifted by President Biden.

In addition to his executive actions, we all know the horrific statements he has made concerning people of color, women, and the LGBTQIAP community. It was the Supreme Court justices that the former President appointed who are responsible for the overturning of Roe v. Wade. Governor Ron DeSantis of Florida, an additional potential candidate for the 2024 presidential election, has already passed countless laws in Florida attacking the LGBTQIAP community; however, he is now using his executive reach to prohibit schools and universities in the state from teaching the history and reality of race in this country.

Under DeSantis's administration, at the time when racial tension sits at an all-time high, the Florida Supreme Court has discontinued diversity training for judges. He has openly condemned and banned an AP African American college course in the state of Florida, banned diversity and inclusivity programs, and now he may run for the highest office in the land. Human rights in the United States would undergo a crushing and devastating blow under a DeSantis administration or another Trump administration, which will put the future of the entire country on thin ice. With everything in our God-given power, we cannot allow this to happen.

We all know the kinds of results of such executive and administrative actions: the public chastisement and humiliation of certain groups of Americans. Due to a negative aspect of our country's history, people of color, women, and the LGBTQIAP community are more susceptible to ridicule, harassment, and discrimination simply because of who they are. Enacting laws that openly undermine their constitutional rights, degrade their livelihood, and limit their ability to function normally in a free society will only increase the prospects for hate crimes and additional acts of domestic terrorism. Given the rising statistics of hate crimes against gays, lesbians, and trans men and trans women, one would assume that individuals such as former President Trump or Governor DeSantis would seek to enact laws cracking down on hate crimes and enhancing federal protections for all Americans, not further scrutinizing marginalized groups.

Given the recent acts of unlawful police murders as well as the civil unrest that follows, one would assume that we all would be trying to come together and have a greater conversation about the reality of race and how we can finally put an end to discriminatory and racially violent practices. One would assume that we all would sit personal politics aside as it pertains to issues that affect the everyday lives and physical well-being of American citizens, and we would do all that is necessary to increase access to employment, adequate healthcare, quality education, and housing. However, most of those on the far right are indeed not, and those who have expressed minimal interest are not taking on the larger, increasingly radical faction of today's Republican Party.

Over the course of our history, our general state of disagreement has always served as a source of strength, not weakness. Our ability to have private discussions at the dinner table, during a drive in the car, or over the phone concerning issues like the economy or national security or climate change has always done us tremendous good, and our greater ability to have a national discussion concerning various economic policy or foreign policy has always led our nation to new heights.

This is what defines democracy. However, no person should ever have to find their self debating another person concerning whether their existence matters. That person should never have to prove to anyone, especially their own government, why they deserve an equal shot at the American Dream as well as access to healthcare or an education or just the mere right to exist and function in everyday society. The fact that I am even having to say that only shows how much we as a country have digressed in the area of equity.

Let us also set more facts straight: the debate concerning human rights for transgender people or the LGBTQIAP community at large has nothing at all to do with harming children or someone imposing a grotesque agenda on our kids. If people like Donald Trump, Ron DeSantis, Marjorie Taylor Greene, and Lauren Boebert were so concerned about protecting our children, they would be doing all that is within their power politically and personally to remind our children why they should love themselves, not hate who they may or may not feel like they truly are deep down inside. They would be doing everything within their authority to ban so-called conversion therapy, which has been linked to greater instances of trauma and higher rates of suicide among children. They would instead be more concerned with increasing access to mental health resources so that adolescents are not left at the mercy of drug addiction, alcoholism, or self-harm.

They would be doing everything in their power to abolish poverty and systemic racism by raising the minimum wage and increasing access to adequate healthcare and education and housing. They would be doing everything they can to get military-style assault weapons and AR-15s out of gun stores and doing everything possible to combat the growing threats of a warming planet. What they would not be doing is seeking to ban life-saving gender-affirming care that so many young Americans need, and they certainly would not be in a twist about drag shows over all the truly evil things that pose a lasting danger to young people today.

If the radical far right in this country was truly concerned about the safety and welfare of our children, they would be more concerned with evil men walking in the streets holding torches shouting, "Jews will not replace us" than with the effort to destroying the lives of ordinary, everyday Americans who are just simply trying to exist without certain others. While she claims to love our children so much, Marjorie Taylor Greene would have never thought to harass adolescent victims of the Parkland shooting while they are walking along the sidewalk just minding their own business. Speaking of Marjorie, she sees calling for the execution of multiple Congressional leaders as exhibiting role model-like behavior for our children. If Ron DeSantis truly cared about the safety of our kids, he would have never scolded a group of high-school kids on live television for wearing COVID masks to protect themselves and others from catching and spreading a deadly virus to the more vulnerable among us.

Marjorie Taylor Greene and Donald Trump certainly would not be co-sponsors of a deadly insurrection on our Capitol to reverse the course of American democracy, injuring and murdering multiple members of law enforcement, referring to the insurrectionists as great patriots, and threatening the lives of the children who happened to be at the Capitol on January 6th if they were seeking truly to protect our kids. By the way, anyone who would compare the justified killing of January 6th Capitol insurrectionist Ashli Babbitt to the unlawful murders of George Floyd and Tyre Nichols has just proven to the world that they do in fact know that systemic racism does exist indeed but will only manipulate the issue for their political advantage.

For one to yell to the world loudly and constantly concerning their love for children is an amazing thing to do, but their behavior in public, how they treat others, and the laws in which they advocate for and support as elected officials tell us all that we must know concerning their character, their position on full equal rights under federal law, and how they feel truly about young people in general.

Terry Schilling, president of the right-wing organization known as the American Principles Project, admitted to CNN that the group's fundamental long-term goal is to eliminate gender-affirming care for Americans of all ages. Mr. Schilling admitted also that the organization works with various states to pass and enact such discriminatory laws. So, again, passing laws to ban gender-affirming care for minors has nothing to do with protecting our kids. It is only a prerequisite for punishing all Americans who identify as either a trans man or trans woman, which will only worsen the stigma against an identity and way of life that is misconstrued broadly. This will only be followed by a rise in the number of hate crimes as well as a decline in mental health and instances of suicide among transgender men and women, particularly among younger Americans.

On the flip side, a study that was published in the New England Journal of Medicine in January 2023 established that transgender youth saw a greater degree of life satisfaction and a decrease in depressive symptoms and anxiety after receiving gender-affirming hormone therapy for two years. The American Medical Association and the American Academy of Pediatrics has classified gender-affirming care as safe and medically necessary for transgender youth and adults.

The good news is that states such as Illinois, California, Massachusetts, Vermont, Connecticut, and Minnesota have enacted laws declaring themselves as sanctuary states for all transgender individuals seeking gender-affirming health care and protects doctors and providers who administer the care. Now, this action must be pursued at the federal level because we are one nation built upon the same ideals, and no individual states should be allowed to trample upon the constitutional rights of any American citizen.

Studies show that gender dysphoria can begin as early as four years old. What I am about to assert is critically important to the long-term well-being of all children: if a child were to approach an educational authority figure or any other adult concerning how they feel, they must be listened to fully. Whether it be gender dysphoria or any other issue of major concern to that child, the adult must take the time to listen to them and hear them. The child must be taken seriously and not be ignored under any circumstance.

When children reach out to others with a situation but are ignored consistently over an extended period, they are likely to become delinquent as they become older. They are likely to break the law and cause harm to others as an attention-seeking mechanism. This is because they were not taken seriously as children. It would be because those they depended on as children to simply be there refused to meet them where they once were.

While a child may still be very young and in the developmental stages of their life, they are still human. They still have thoughts, emotions, and concerns, and are still capable of experiencing trauma. There are also many minors who have expressed desire or interest in obtaining gender-affirming care who have the full support of their parents. All those who would consider this an act of child abuse are truly ignorant of the issue and need to undergo thorough research before making uneducated assumptions concerning a very complicated subject matter. In addition to conversion therapy, what would be considered child abuse from any adult is refusing to extend to a child both the physical and emotional support they require.

The right-wing extremists who would subjugate parents to legal consequences just to forward a political agenda because those parents choose to support their children through critical gender-affirming care should be highly ashamed. The same extremists will go to bat for a child before they are even born but will vanish completely once the child has entered the world and requires more support than they could ever ask for. If so many of us continue to make conclusions based on personal feelings and fear rather than do our research on this deeply complex and complicated issue, the consequences on our children will be detrimental.

It is imperative for every child to have avenues in which to turn to express their thoughts, feelings, and concerns. If a child is experiencing gender dysphoria, it does not imply anything negative concerning who the child is as a person in general. Gender dysphoria can occur at any age; this is why society need to listen to science and pursue research so we can all achieve a greater understanding of these kinds of complicated situations. This will enable us to better care for and understand our children.

Again, the only kind of individuals who would assert that "individuals can change their gender all they want but just keep it away from my children" are probably those who are harboring layers of transphobia in their hearts, which should never define how we respond to our children and should not dictate the contents of public policy under any circumstance. Based on all that we have seen so far, ranging from the proposal of over three-hundred discriminatory laws throughout the country to a significant rise in hate crimes, the radical far right in this country is not remotely interested in helping our children or preventing child abuse; their goal is restricting the human rights of anyone who is not white, straight, cisgender, and male.

I am someone who has worked with children for eight years as an educator at both the elementary and secondary school grade levels, fourteen years as a motivational speaker, eleven years as an anti-bullying and suicide prevention advocate, and now as a college admissions advisor. My entire career has revolved around assisting young people in overcoming adversities and achieving their greatest potential. I have always done everything in my power to ensure the safety and betterment of every child in which I have served and held responsibility for. To suggest that the effort to establish full equal rights under the law for all Americans is a threat to our children is not only absurd but a complete and grave insult to not only myself but to every parent and all those who have nothing but love and adoration at heart for all children.

All those who would conjure up such a false and bogus claim should apologize to not only the rest of us but the entire nation. Furthermore, no person in this country should ever be forced to uproot their life from one state to another because their home state refuses to recognize their worth and constitutional freedoms as an American citizen. That is not who we are. We are the United States of America with liberty and justice for all, not just those who seem to satisfy shallow standards of perfection. This threat against human rights in our country is more detrimental and serious than ever before, and all of us need to start doing something about it. MAGA will not stop until we stop them.

So, the question before us is very simple: how do we stop them? What must we as citizens do to preserve and protect the human dignity of every American, regardless of background? The first and important thing we must do is vote. We must vote our hearts out in every election like we never have before. We must vote up and down the ticket from president all the way down to city or town council. The second thing we must do is gather up our families and friends, ensure they are registered to vote, and get them to the polls as well. The third thing is to volunteer and organize on behalf of candidates who pledge to fight tooth and nail for the human rights all citizens. Fourth and finally, we should consider running for office ourselves.

As a former candidate for office myself, I endured the hawk of the freezing cold as well as unbearable heat and consistent exhaustion while canvassing each day of the campaign season, but what kept me going was reminding myself all the time that the result in the end would be worth it. The stakes now in our country are higher than they have ever been, and we must extend a positive voice to every heartbeat of discouragement, disappointment, and void. We must use that voice to create positive change as did those who came before us. If we do all that is necessary to reverse this effort to take us back to 1950 and lead a new generation to the future, America, it will be worth it. This is our time to protect the dignity and respect of all of God's children, no matter who they are, how they look, or how they live.

As stated earlier, this debate consists of far more than mere disagreements on issues pertaining to the economy, education, tax rates, and offshore drilling. The issue of full equal rights under federal law is a life-or-death issue, and we have a moral and sacred obligation to put this profound threat to our sole fact of existence behind us. Generations before us fought and sacrificed all in which they had for everyday of their lives so that we in our generation and future generations would never have to endure the agonies of the past.

Too many Americans have been mistreated, too many Americans have suffered to the fullest, and too many Americans have died unlawfully for any of us to sit back and allow this dangerous tirade of injustice to continue any longer. Instead of manufacturing baseless and bogus justifications in our minds to bully and constantly attack the human rights of those who are different from we are, ripping apart at the lives of so many people, why not apply that fundamentally unconditional love for God that so many of claim to have and search deep within our spirit for the infinite reasons why not to roll back equal protections for all under the law and desecrate the lives and livelihoods of marginalized groups of the population? Would Christ Himself bestow evil into the lives of those who are different from Him, or would He love them without error and demonstrate that love through His everyday actions and behavior?

In the year 2023, no American of any race, any gender, any sexual orientation, or any gender identity should ever be subjected to bigotry, discrimination, or hate of any kind. In 2023, no citizen of the United States of America should be suffering to the point of death in the Twenty-first Century due to the practices and tendencies of the past. White supremacy and toxic masculinity have negatively impacted just about every aspect of our lives, our culture, and our politics for far too long, and they should no longer dictate any aspect of American law and public policy. Our profound dignity as human beings and as the children of God must be guarded consistently and heavily so that the wrath of injustice, inspired only by the sin of pure hate, no longer has influence over our collective humanity evermore.

American democracy belongs to us all, and the time is now to end the mass influence of radical far right extremists forever, and all the co-conspiring right-wing violent extremists should be prosecuted to the full extent of American justice and thrown into prison. The time to honor the respectful treatment of all Americans from every walk of life is now. If we fail to seize this golden opportunity at this very moment to do what we know in our hearts is decent and what will bring healing to a divided nation, there may come a time when it is too late. Time's up! That's it. Enough is enough! America, our time is now.

4

Could A Historical Blue Wave be Just What America Needs?

'The Republican Party's version of the country is a portrait of privilege; ours is a mirror of America."
--Vice-President Walter Mondale

It is apparent that both political parties have edged unusually far in their prospective directions. Both the Democratic Party and the Republican Party look tremendously different today from twenty-years ago and even from just a decade ago. Just between fifteen and ten years ago today, President Obama, who has inspired me to the fullest and whom I admire wholeheartedly, would have been referred to by some as a hardcore liberal. According to today's political standards, however, he is now seen by many as a moderate. While it may be inaccurate, some may even designate President Clinton as a moderate conservative. Notable liberals of today of whom I look up to would include Senators Bernie Sanders and Elizabeth Warren, Representative Alexandria Ocasio-Cortez, and Governors Gavin Newsom of California and J.B. Pritzker of my home state, Illinois.

As a strong and proud Democrat, I am not ashamed to admit that my own party has shifted towards the left to a fair amount over the past few years. This is only due, however, to various issues taking place throughout the country. Issues such as civil unrest, racial injustice, systemic injustice against women and the LGBTQIAP community, and increasing rates of poverty and joblessness can have drastic effects on a nation's politics. Even as my party has shifted to an adequate extent, I remain an unashamed member of the Democratic Party who will support my party wholeheartedly because of its ideals and solutions to longstanding problems that must be solved immediately. In another aspect, I pray that the Democrats' great migration to the left is an indication that we will never compromise on the sole issues of voting rights, racial justice, women's rights, LGBTQIAP equality under federal law, and closing the widening gap between the rich and the poor.

When it comes to the Republican Party, something is happening that exceeds ideological boundaries. The problem in the former party of Lincoln is more than just an adequate shift to the right. What is taking place is an embracing of something so radical and un-American that it has become beyond unrecognizable. For over forty years, the party has embraced ideas that are profoundly out of touch with the everyday, common American such as massive tax breaks for the top one percent, endless military spending that is not required to keep us safe, gutting essential services for those in dire need, rolling back environmental protections, vouchers for charter schools, and a refusal to reform our gun laws.

These ideas have always proven themselves reckless for America since day one. Historically, they have produced massive budget deficits over short periods of time, an increase in the overall national debt, widespread economic recessions, wider gaps between the rich and poor, increased rates of child hunger, failing schools, and a weaker position on the global stage. Once again, however, today's Republican Party is focused on something far more dangerous and completely anathema to all that has defined America's greatness since 1776.

Rather than pursue a broad, two-way discussion in our country concerning common issues that affect citizens from both sides of the aisle alike, Republican leaders across the nation have embraced a dangerously radical position that dismisses the reality of the everyday American. Instead, they have insisted on initiating pointless culture wars that is a complete political turn-off to most Americans, particularly the younger generation.

Republican leaders at both the federal and state levels are imposing an unwanted and dangerous cultural agenda that only stands to worsen our nation's depressive state of division. Issues such as mental health, racial equity, access to safe abortions and contraception, rightful access to gender-affirming care at all ages followed by all that comes with it, and overhauling America's broken gun laws at the federal level resonate deeply with the hearts of so many young Americans and their parents.

The younger generation desires access to an affordable college education, the means to finance it, and student-loan forgiveness. There are also issues that are unique to people of color such as systemic racism as well as disproportionate access to the American Dream, including certain economic opportunities, adequate healthcare, quality education, fair housing, and safety. The relationship between people of color and law enforcement has certainly reached the center of the current state of public affairs. There are also the issues of higher pay for teachers, strengthening Social Security and Medicare, and lowering the costs of prescription drugs and insulin.

All the issues discussed above are deeply important to countless Americans. The great people of this country go above and beyond each day in doing the basic things just to survive. They strive diligently every day of their lives as the average cost of living continues to increase substantially over time at no fault of their own. As America continues through economic hardship, there are many who wonder how they will pay the bills or the mortgage, put food on the table, and send their kids to college. Many Americans worry non-stop concerning how or if they will make it through these troubling times and achieve greater stability.

Given all the fundamental difficulties of the current day, how in the world can today's Republican Party insist on ignoring the reality of our time and carrying forward with inferior-based culture wars that no one wants and that will not bestow anything positive upon the American people? How will eroding the constitution, attacking human rights endlessly, and imposing an authoritarian overreach serve the best interests of the average American seeking a better life for them and their children? It simply will not.

If something positive does come out of this pointless hidden agenda, it will be only for a narrowing electoral base that do not speak for a new and growingly diverse generation of Americans. Today's Republican Party has insisted also on carrying forward former President Trump's big lie concerning the 2020 presidential election. It has been twenty-six months since the election; why hasn't the party moved on? Why hasn't the party attempted to embrace a vision for the future?

Why hasn't the party tried to put forth meaningful ideas and prospective solutions to the everyday problems of Americans instead of dwelling on past political failures? Why hasn't today's Republican Party overall condemned and moved on from Donald J. Trump? If former President Trump himself cared anything about his party or the entire country for that matter, he would put his grievances concerning his loss behind him like so many past leaders and mature human beings have always done and seek to unite the country based on a vision we can all rally behind. However, since he pledged to "fan the flame" of his loss by insisting on a revenge tour as part of his third presidential attempt, followed by his party's commitment to support him if he is the party's nominee next year, both he and his party have proven no desire or wish to listen to the American people and move us all forward.

So, what is the best starting point for America going forward? Given the recent trend of events, it would have to be an historical blue wave. Specifically, at least a Democratic 60-40 super majority in the Senate, a solid Democratic majority in the House, and, of course, maintaining a Democratic Commander-in-Chief. This will allow us to accomplish vital long overdue tasks such as overhauling voting rights, passing the Equality Act, codifying abortion rights and a woman's autonomy over her own body and healthcare into federal law, enacting reasonable and common-sense police reform, requiring universal background checks and an age limit of 21 to purchase a firearm, banning assault weapons once and for all, increasing the national minimum wage to at least $15/hr., instituting high-speed rail, making the first two years of college in this country free of charge to prospective students, enacting higher pay for teachers, instituting a Medicare-for-All healthcare option at the federal level, and passing the CROWN Act. There are many additional things that must be done as well.

Today's Republican Party leadership has proven itself unwilling to have a meaningful, mature debate concerning important issues affecting Americans and offering meaningful solutions, and they continue to stand oblivious to any reality beyond that of their own. Their only responses to the critical issues of our time consist of the same typical slander: "that's gonna raise taxes," "stop trying to make us more like Europe," "stop whining about the past," "guns do not kill people; people kill people," "you're a baby killer," "gays and trans people are perverts," "immigrants are taking over America," "I don't want my kids exposed to that," "you hate this country," "go back to from where you came," "that's the media making us look bad," or "that's fake news!"

The reality is this: Americans have had enough of the consistent malice, constant bullying, willful ignorance, finger-pointing, and unsubstantial nonsense as usual from our Republican friends, and this was made quite evident during the 2022 midterm elections. Having a hard time rejecting what is evil and refusing to stand firm for what is logically and morally right disqualifies them from the majority.

Were we really surprised when the parents of slain officers from the January 6th Capitol insurrection refused to shake Senate Minority

Leader Mitch McConnell's because his party's leadership on Capitol Hill chose politics over holding the mastermind accountable? Was the nation shocked to witness our Republican friends perform so poorly during the midterm elections in 2022? The American people spoke loudly and clearly, as they always do.

This night should have been a fundamental wake-up call to every single Republican lawmaker in Washington to shift course drastically, not for the mere sake of winning elections but as a reminder of what the American people have been trying to tell them for quite some time. It is beyond difficult to conduct the people's work when one of our major parties continues to apply endless obstructionist methods. It is harder to solve longstanding challenges that continue to have a tremendous impact on so many American lives.

We have reached a milestone in American politics where many of us have begun to question whether current Republican Party leadership will ever get on board with the rest of the country and reject toxic governance as well as rising political figures who pose a profound threat to life in America as we know it to be. Patriotism consists of far greater than just merely articulating a love of country; it is carried out through the acts of leadership and moral character, putting country first in the example of the late distinguished senator from Arizona, John McCain, and presenting no quarrel against holding extremists and dictator-wannabe political figures accountable no matter the cost. I am not only advocating for a massive blue wave like we have never seen, but I am issuing a call to all those traditional establishment Republican voters who have been disillusioned and demoralized by the extreme direction in which their long-known party has gone and is attempting to take the entire country.

Traditional establishment Republican voters are no different from most of us; they simply work hard each day to give their families a greater life; they desire safe communities, an adequate education system, and affordable healthcare as well as a closer aim at the American Dream overall. They shout thanks to God each morning they wake up and each night before bedtime. They go to church, pay their taxes, and do their best to instill the basic values of honesty, character, and respect into their children. More than anything else, they yearn for a government that works on their behalf and not the other way around. I say to each one of them: the Democratic Party hears you; we see you; we see clearly how the Republican Party of today has let you down and abandoned you in all those areas disgracefully, and we have much better to offer.

We know that you love this country as much as the rest of us; we will never question your patriotism due to mere political dissonance; while you may still have your conservative worldview, which we respect wholeheartedly, we welcome you with open arms to our side, and we pledge to move our country forward together if you choose to join us. Rather than lead America down a dangerous path of consistent partisan obstruction, endless culture wars, baseless and deadly conspiracy theories, and violent political extremism, the Democratic Party stands steadfast and ready to address the rising challenges of an awakened new generation, meet the concerns and needs of everyday families, and unite America based on common hopes and a single shaped destiny. Rather than declare enemies out of those who simply disagree with us, we pledge to embrace our disagreements, strengthen democracy, never stop fighting until the fight is won, and put forth an agenda that will lift all citizens because at the end of the day, we are citizens of the United States of America. Join us and let us move this country forward.

Conclusion

"The best way to destroy an enemy is to make him a friend."

--President Abraham Lincoln

What is happening in America today is something to the lights of which has never taken place: America is waking up. A new generation of Americans is waking up to unfortunate realities that have become worse for quite some time now such as systemic injustice against people of color, women of all backgrounds, and the LGBTQIAP community. Additional realities include the gap between the rich and poor, climate change, gun violence, widespread poverty, and mental illness. There are also those attempting to take us back to the 1950s when the white straight cisgender male paradigm defined the cultural and moral standard of that time in history. This was a time when anyone who did not fulfill that standard was not only deemed inferior but treated as such in every possible way. These same individuals are attempting to silence our generation when we speak out against it.

Our nation is at a crossroads like never before. There are one or two paths we can choose; we can enter a common path and embrace the ideals and principles upon which have always defined our nation's success. We can come together on the same page to solve long overdue issues that have greatly affected and harmed so many lives. We can unite, chart a bold course for the future, embrace a transforming and growing generation, and put an end to an outdated, warn out brand of thinking that only seeks to hold us back. We can embrace the good in ourselves and seek out the good in others, or we can continue the path we are on right now.

We can continue to embrace the white supremacist hold of the past and avoid the required conversations about race and the unfortunate reality surrounding it. We can continue to embrace toxic masculine standards by taking women for granted and dismissing their struggles, followed by a continued tirade of profound injustice and mass scrutiny of those who identify as gay, lesbian, bisexual, and transgender. We can continue to belittle one another because of our differences in political and ideological views, preventing much-needed progress on a host of important challenges that have lingered for generations. Lastly, we can keep on with the same nonsensical business we have been conducting for a very long time that will only push us farther and farther apart until we can no longer see each other at all.

If we continue in this dangerous direction, there will be civil war in this country to the lights of which we have never seen. Instead of just our feelings being hurt, there will be people hurt physically and permanently. Instead of just some of us giving up on voting and politics overall, there will be some who may lose their lives altogether. This will forever dismantle the state of democracy and alter the course of humanity for generations to come. None of us should want this; all of us should desire a nation where we are all respected fully and where we honor each other's presence.

We should all desire a country where we can live in stability, peacefully being able to conduct the everyday business of our nation on behalf of our posterity. This future can be won if all of us did our part and simply do our best to refrain from chastising those who are different and stop being so politically obstructive towards one another. Let us stop trying to return to the way things were; let us move forward because forward is the only way and the best way to go. If this nation delves into civil war, may God forbid heavily, it will do so because of those who continuously and consistently tried time and time again to take us back to 1950. It will be due to those who sought to overthrow American democracy and seize power to the point of authoritarian, if not totalitarian, control and domination.

We will enter civil war because too many among us would have failed to see the bigger picture in all aspects because they were too concerned with their own feelings, their own narrow perspective of reality, and their imposition of that narrow reality as well as the intolerance that follows. Continuing to forsake our collective American spirit will send this nation into a tailspin from which we may not be able to escape. Our collective humanity flourishes when we first condemn the false narratives meant to hold us back and set our eye on a future of limitless possibilities.

Prior to the signing of the Emancipation Proclamation to end the physical captivity of slavery, there were many African American slaves who plotted their escape from bondage. Those who have studied history knows very well that fleeing from captivity was never easy to accomplish. In fact, the consequences were often brutal and deadly if runaway slaves were to be caught by their captors. When heroic freedom soldiers such as Harriet Tubman and a gentleman by the name of Josiah Henson led the escape to freedom, they applied a special strategy called "signal songs." Most of us refer to them as freedom songs. One of the most famous songs they sang was entitled "Follow the Drinking Gourd." The drinking gourd was a code reference to the Big Dipper. This constellation is used to find the North Star.

For the slaves, following the North Star was crucial because the practice of slavery was not prevalent in northern states as it had been in the South. As a result, the runaway slaves fled their way north. Because Tubman and Henson were able to rally the slaves towards a common destination and because they did not turn back, the unthinkable gift of freedom became a new reality for countless African Americans who would be slaves no longer. What led them to freedom was their relentless focus on a shared dream with a common goal; they never took their eye off the heavens; they did not blink when they saw the eye of God.

To all Americans: black and white, Democrat and Republican, Hispanic and Latino, Asian and native, young and old, rich and poor, gay and straight, cisgender and transgender, let us not blink at the eye of God. Let us all set our laser sights on that North Star, follow that path steadfast and persistently, and never relent until that shared American Dream becomes a new American reality for us all. We must not stop until that common goal of a more perfect union has been fulfilled and passed on to a new generation.

We must never appease nor concede to those calling for our nation's demise just so they can capitalize on political power. Let us heed the example of the many great individuals who came before us. Let us once again summon that formidable, unspeakable collective spirit of our nation that can never be compromised nor defeated. As we look up towards the heavens and lock humanity's eye onto the mighty eye of God, we will then look up again and look at our surroundings and realize suddenly that we the American people for the first time in history are running hand-in-hand in the same direction together singing "Follow the Drinking Gourd." America, follow the drinking gourd!

www.ingramcontent.com/pod-product-compliance
Lightning Source LLC
Chambersburg PA
CBHW071224260726
48653CB00042B/2216